Ready, steady, Go!

Dave Boyle
Wendy Pitt

CAMBRIDGE UNIVERSITY PRESS

Published by the Press Syndicate of the University of Cambridge
The Pitt Building, Trumpington Street, Cambridge CB2 1RP
40 West 20th Street, New York, NY 10011-4211, USA
10 Stamford Road, Oakleigh, Victoria 3166, Australia

In association with Staffordshire County Council

© Cambridge University Press 1992

First published 1992

Printed in Great Britain by Scotprint Ltd, Musselburgh

Designed and Produced by Gecko Limited, Bicester, Oxon.

A catalogue record of this book is available from the British Library.

ISBN 0 521 40627 7

PICTURE ACKNOWLEDGEMENTS

Christopher Coggins 7c, 8b, 12tr, 12br, 13tl, 13tr, 13br, 15tr, 18, 26, 30.
Robert Harding Picture Library 7tr, 7br.
Images 13bl.
Valiant Technology Ltd. 21.
N Wright/National Motor Museum 8t.
Zefa Ltd. 11, 12bl, 15tl, 15br, 24

Picture Research by Linda Proud

NOTICE TO TEACHERS

The contents of this book are in the copyright of Cambridge University Press. Unauthorised copying of any of the pages is not only illegal but also goes against the interests of the authors.

For authorised copying please check that your school has a licence (through the Local Education Authority) from the Copyright Licensing Agency which enables you to copy small parts of the text in limited numbers.

Contents

Ready, Steady, Go!   **4**

Steering in the right direction   **12**

Production lines   **22**

Ready, Steady Go

Talking together

How many different ways of moving things can you see in the picture?

How are they different?
How are they the same?

How would you describe the way they move?
What makes them move?
Do you know any other ways to move things?

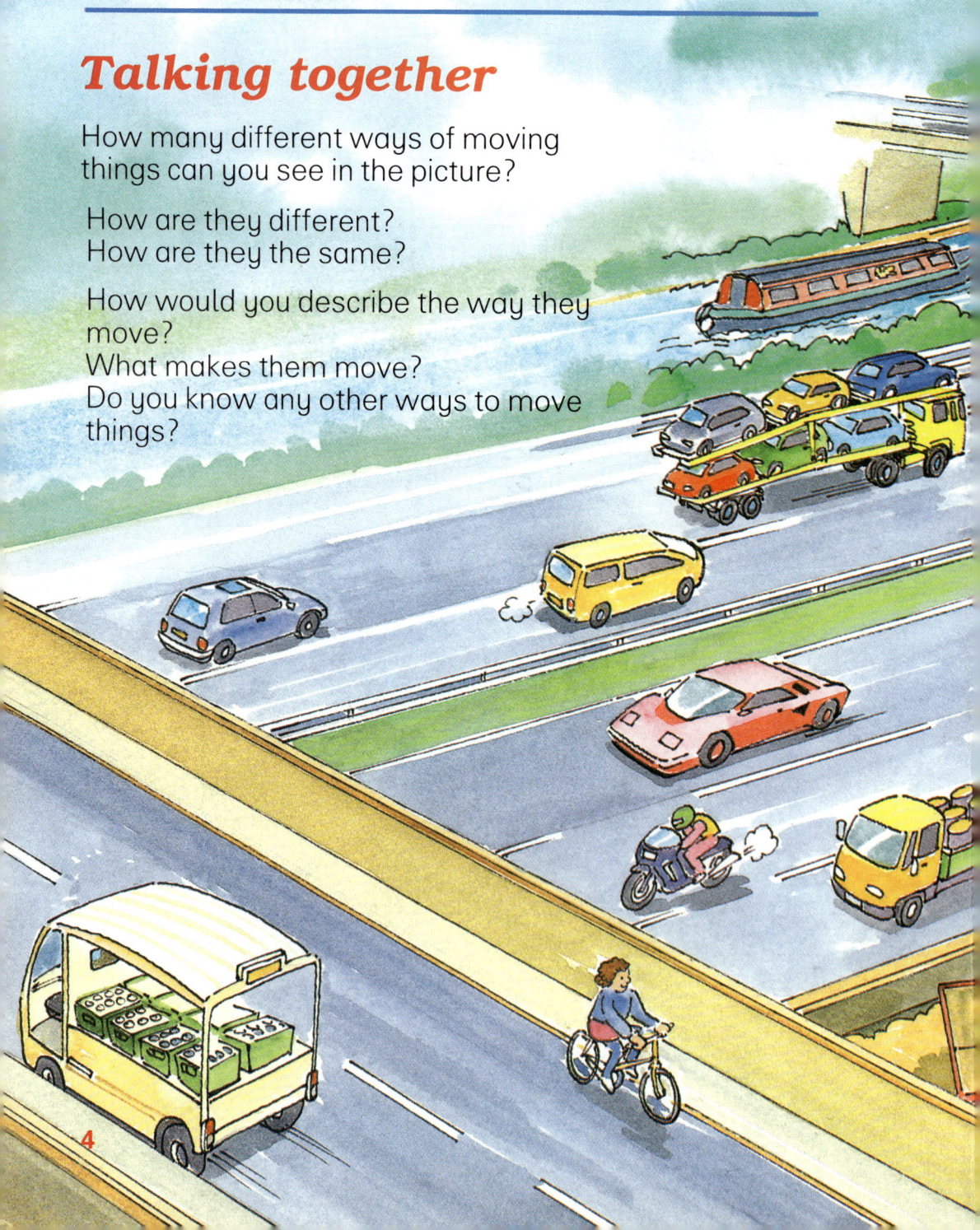

Make a display that shows different methods of moving things from place to place.

The need

The younger children at your school would like a large road layout to play with. They also need some model vehicles which they can play with on the road layout.

Developing your design

Planning your work

What sort of vehicles would the younger children like to play with?

How big are the roads?
How big will the vehicles need to be?
Will the children like to carry some of their toys in the vehicle?

Will this affect your design?

Working parts such as doors, winches and tipping mechanisms may make the vehicles more interesting.

Carry out a survey to find out what sort of models will need to be made.

• DATA FILE •
Card and paper: mechanisms
Research: data collection and display

7

Try different methods of making a simple chassis. Consider different ways of attaching axles to your chassis.

The chassis is the basic framework of the vehicle.

• DATA FILE •

Movement:
axles and chassis

Experiment with wheels of different types.

• DATA FILE •

Movement:
wheels

Try different ways of powering your vehicles.

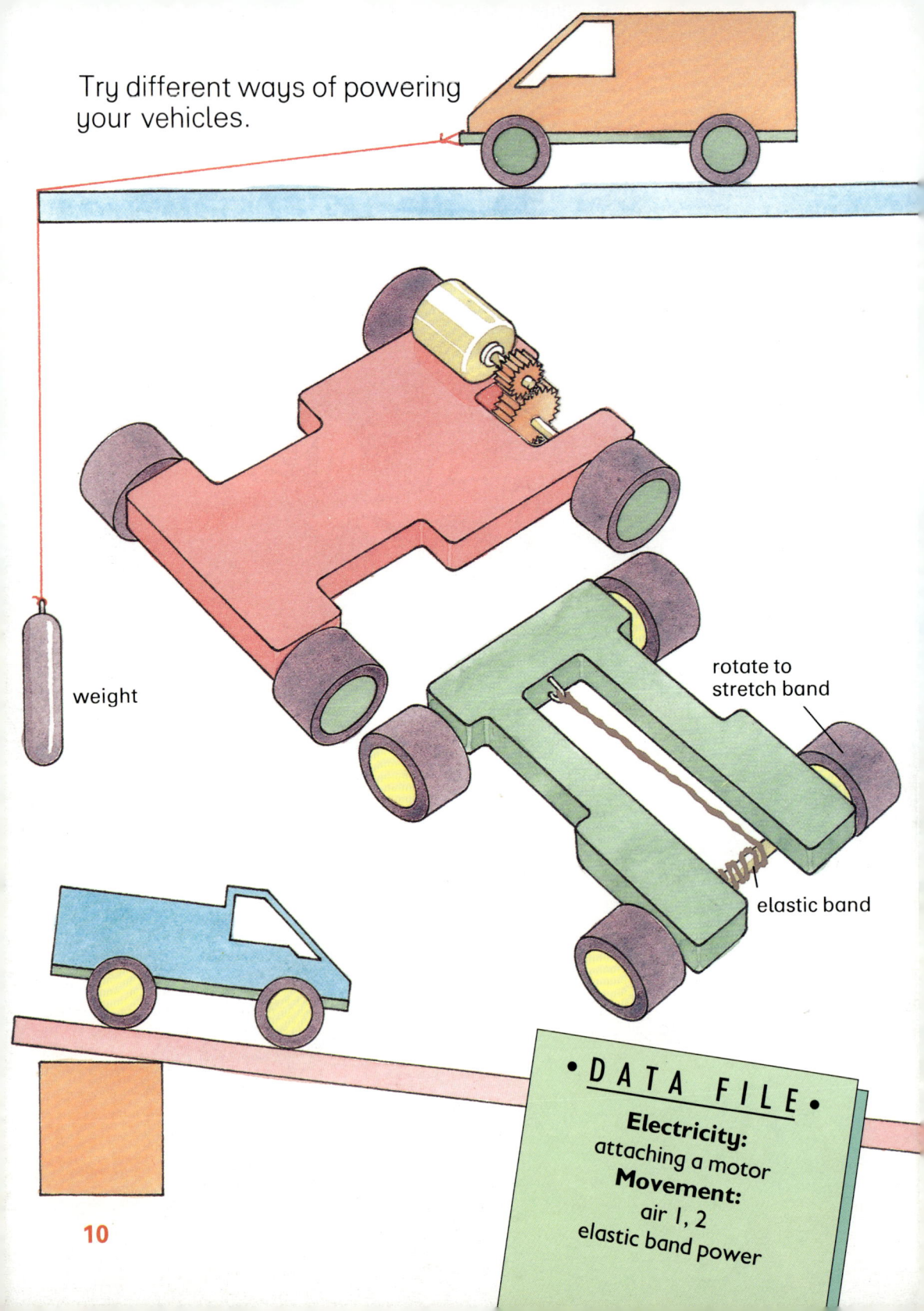

weight

rotate to stretch band

elastic band

• D A T A   F I L E •

Electricity:
attaching a motor
Movement:
air 1, 2
elastic band power

Other ideas

Design a vehicle which can carry a load to the top of a slope.

Make a vehicle which could be used on motorways to warn other drivers of traffic hold-ups.

Design a vehicle which has many safety features.

Design the ultimate luxury vehicle.

Design a vehicle which could be used to carry things over rough ground.

Steering in the right direction

Talking together

Look at the mechanisms and vehicles in the pictures.

What do they do?

How do they work?

How are they controlled?

What different methods are there for doing this?
Why is it important to control these mechanisms accurately?

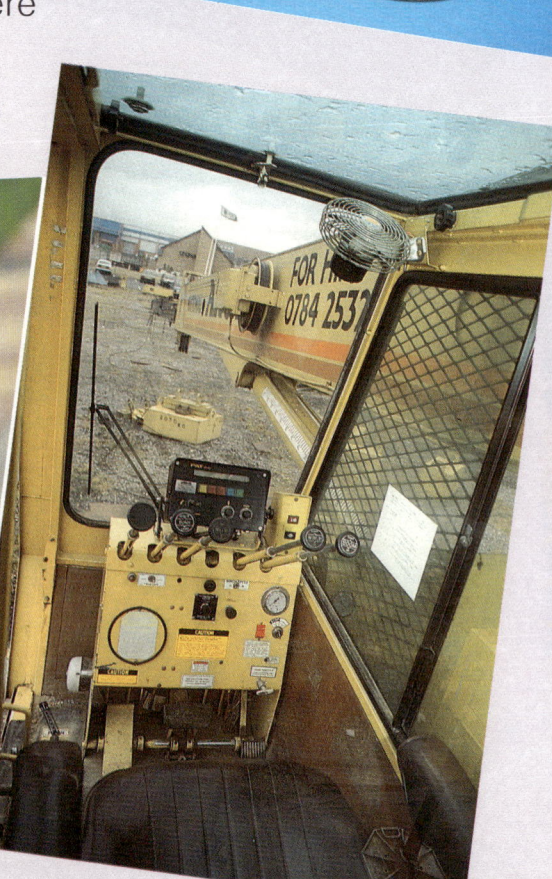

Can you think of any other examples where close control is necessary?

13

The need

Vehicles need to be steered in the right direction and around obstacles. As your models do not have steering mechanisms, you will need to modify them so that they can change direction when necessary.

Developing your design

Planning your ideas

Which different mechanisms could you use to steer your vehicle?
Can you simply add a steering mechanism to your vehicle or do you have to rebuild it?

Do you need to use pivots, linkages or levers?
Do you need power? If so, where will it come from?
Would a hydraulic system be useful?

Use a construction kit to try out your ideas and to find some new ones.

•DATA FILE•
Movement:
vehical steering mechanisms

15

Pivots

Use a simple pivot.

pivot

string

pivot

string

•DATA FILE•
Card and paper:
mechanisms

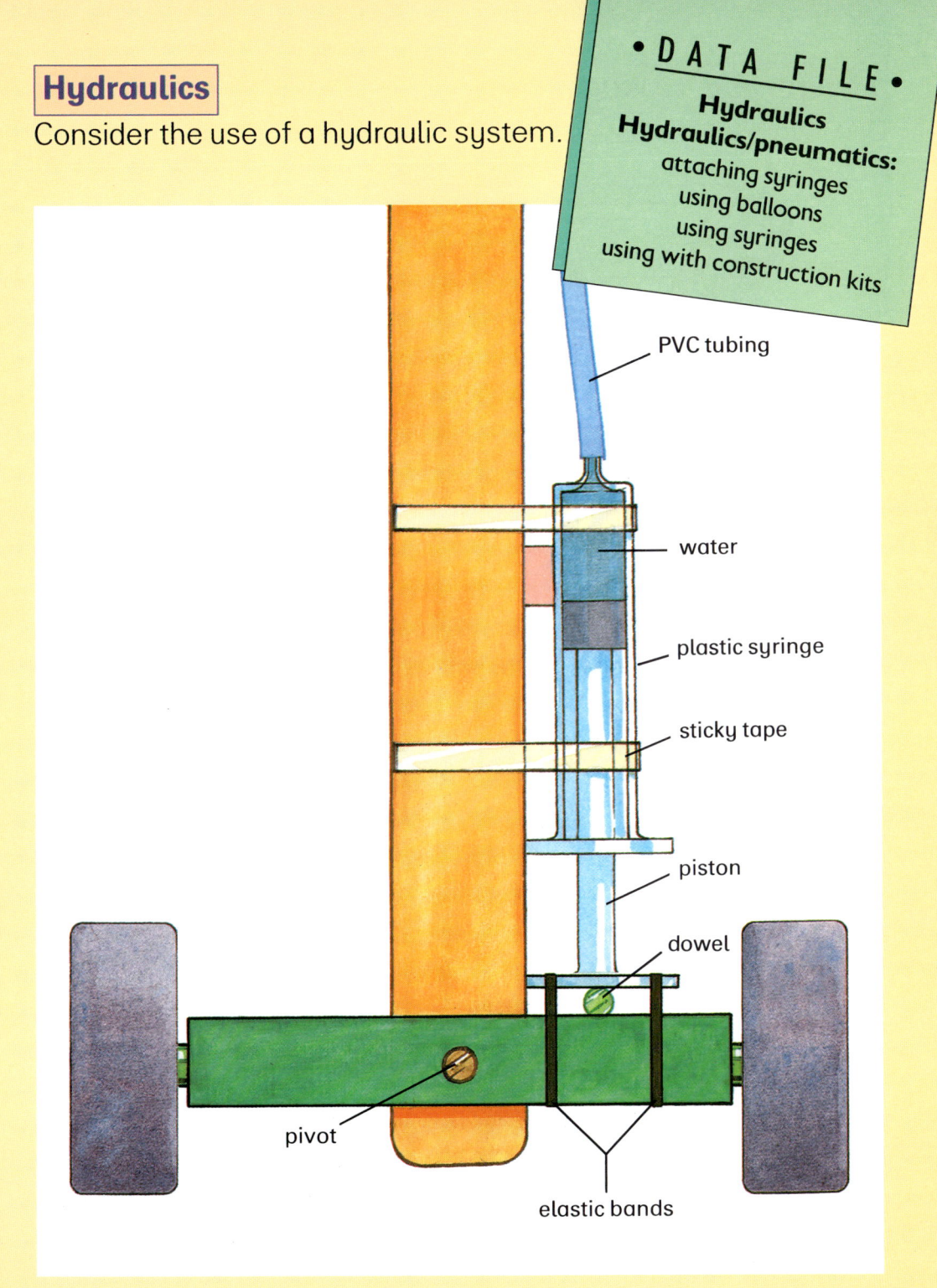

Hydraulics

Consider the use of a hydraulic system.

• D A T A   F I L E •

Hydraulics
Hydraulics/pneumatics:
attaching syringes
using balloons
using syringes
using with construction kits

- PVC tubing
- water
- plastic syringe
- sticky tape
- piston
- dowel
- pivot
- elastic bands

17

Levers and Linkages

Use levers and linkages.

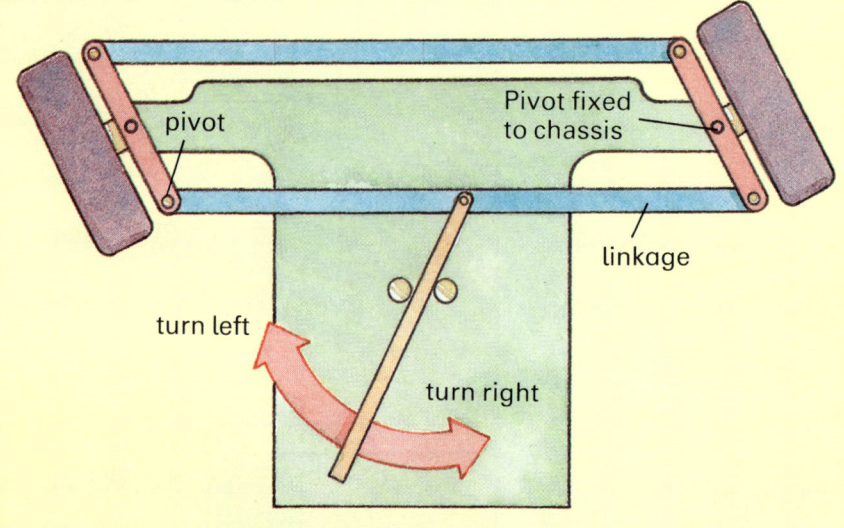

pivot

Pivot fixed to chassis

linkage

turn left

turn right

· D A T A   F I L E ·

Mechanisms: linkages

Rack and pinion

Use a rack and pinion mechanism.

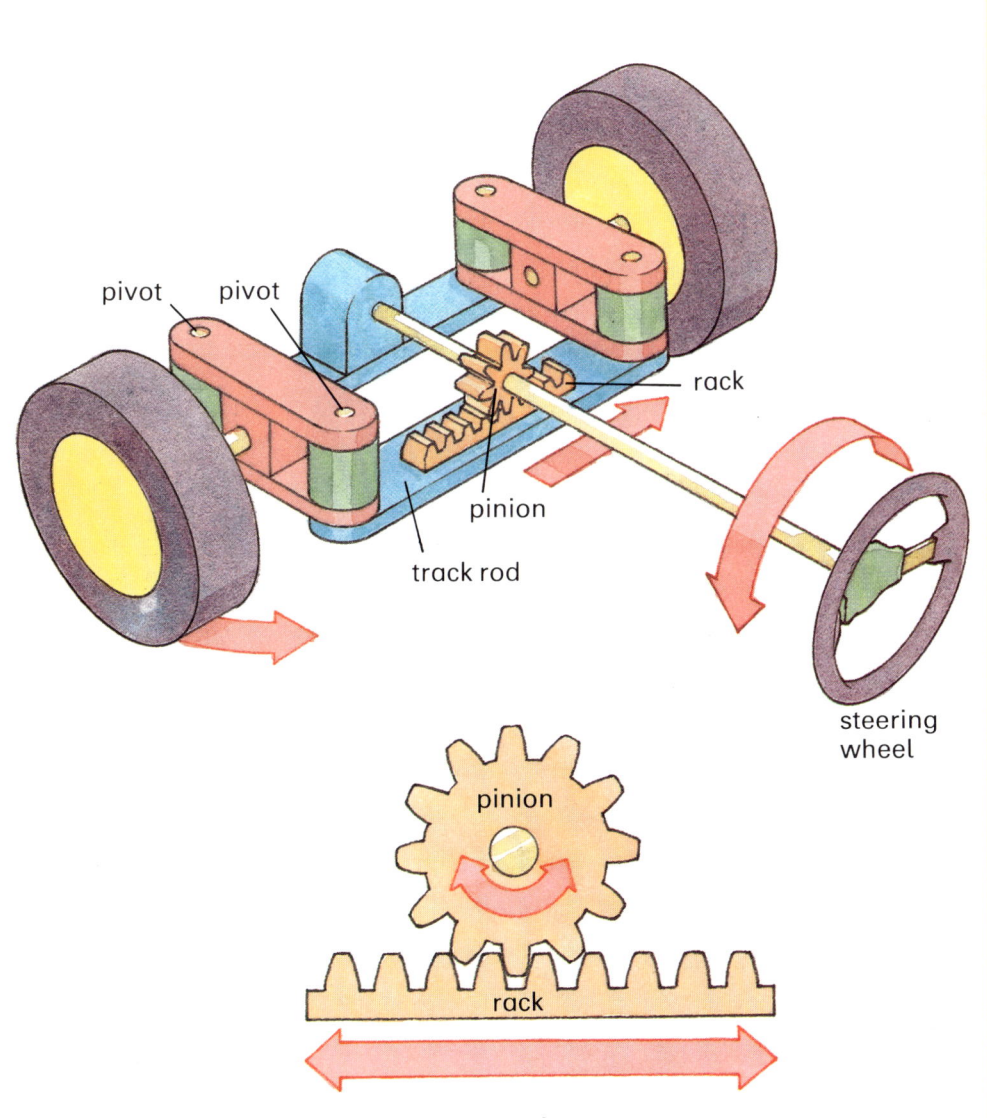

As the steering wheel is turned anti-clockwise the pinion pulls the rack to the right. This moves the linkage and wheels as shown.

• DATA FILE •
Movement:
vehicle steering mechanisms

19

Power

Power the driving wheels separately.

When the right-hand motor moves the front right wheel forward, the vehicle turns left.

To switching unit manually or computer operated

Tracked vehicles use this method of steering

Other ideas

Make a control unit which will let you to steer your model from a distance.

If your model is electrically driven find out how to connect it up to a computer and write a program to operate it.

Design an obstacle course that will test how well you can steer your vehicles.

Production

Talking together

What is happening in the picture?
What is being made?

How many jobs are being done? What are they?
Why are there so many different tasks?
Why are machines being used?

Have you seen a production line in action?
What sort of things are made on a production line?

Lines

Many of the things we see and use every day have been made on a production line. Make a display of objects which may have been made in this way.

The need

Imagine a car manufacturer has heard of the success of your vehicle making. They invite you to visit them to see their production lines. You could raise some funds by making more vehicles using the mass production methods of the factory.

• D A T A   F I L E •
Planning a production line

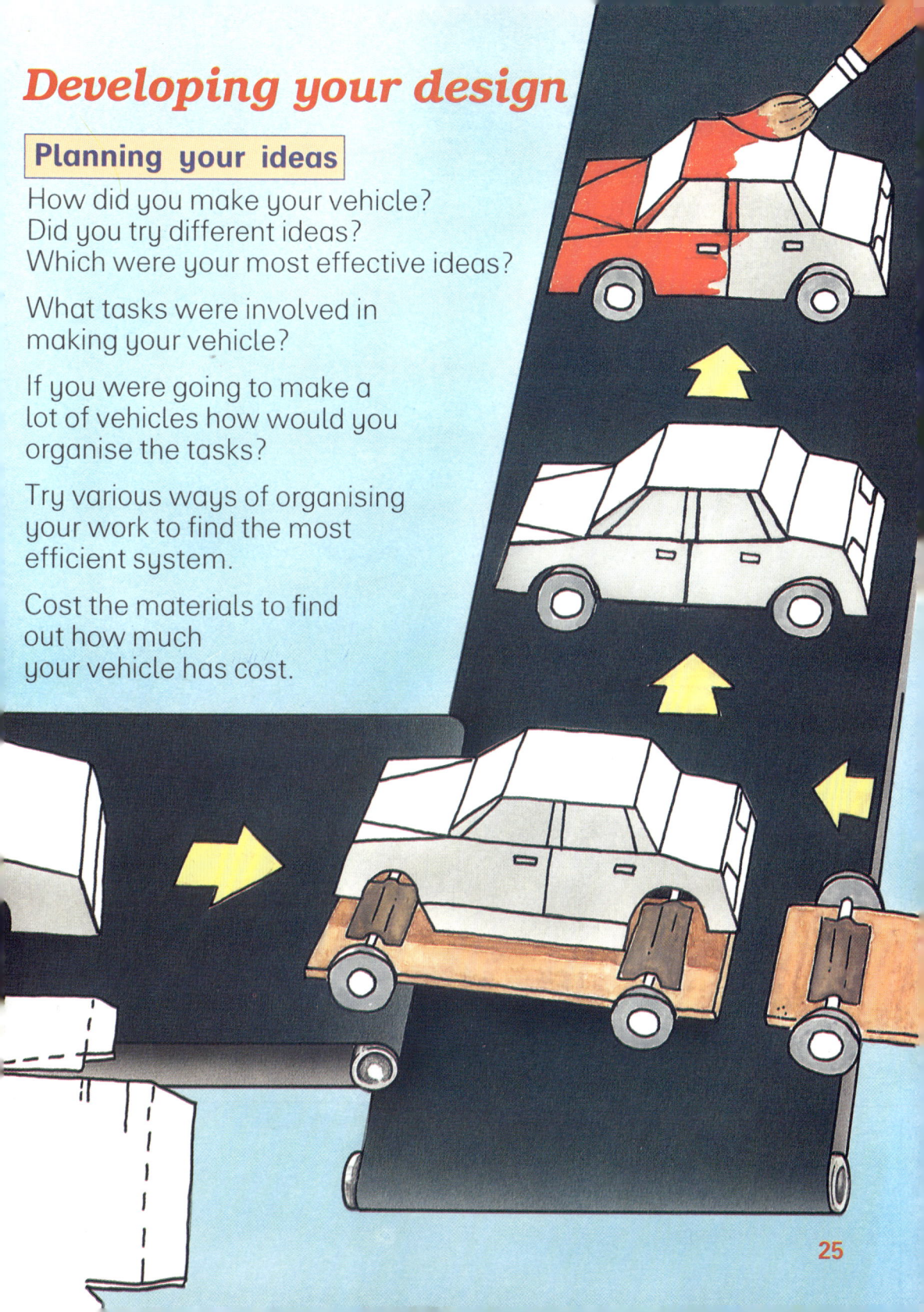

Developing your design

Planning your ideas

How did you make your vehicle?
Did you try different ideas?
Which were your most effective ideas?

What tasks were involved in making your vehicle?

If you were going to make a lot of vehicles how would you organise the tasks?

Try various ways of organising your work to find the most efficient system.

Cost the materials to find out how much your vehicle has cost.

Would it be possible to put different body shells onto one chassis design?

How will you make the body shells?
How will they be attached to the chassis?
Will they need to be decorated?

basic chassis

card body shells

• D A T A   F I L E •
Finishes

A production system

Devise a production line system.

•DATA FILE•
Planning a production line

Bodywork

Make a 3D structure.

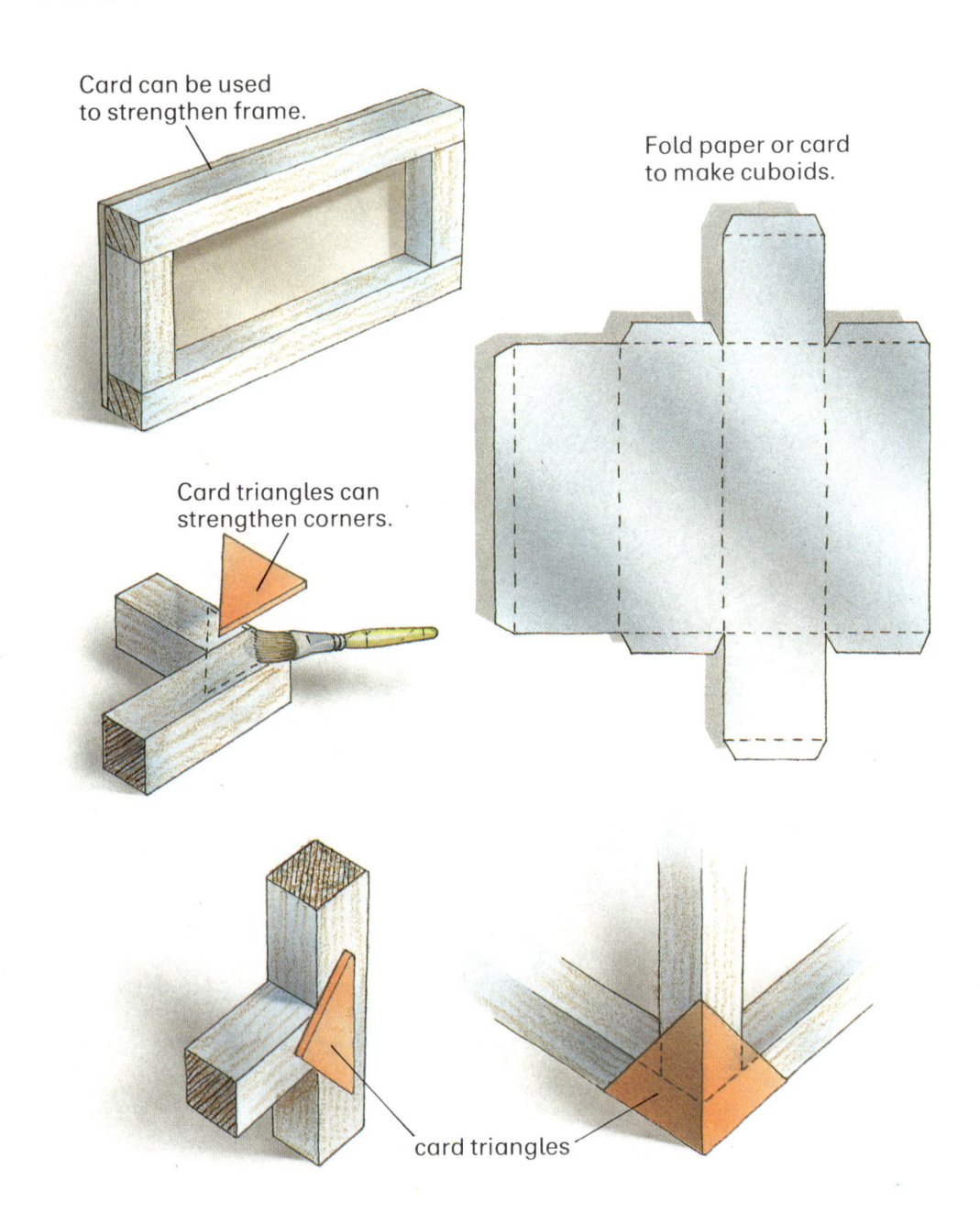

Card can be used to strengthen frame.

Fold paper or card to make cuboids.

Card triangles can strengthen corners.

card triangles

Consider how to attach the body to the chassis.

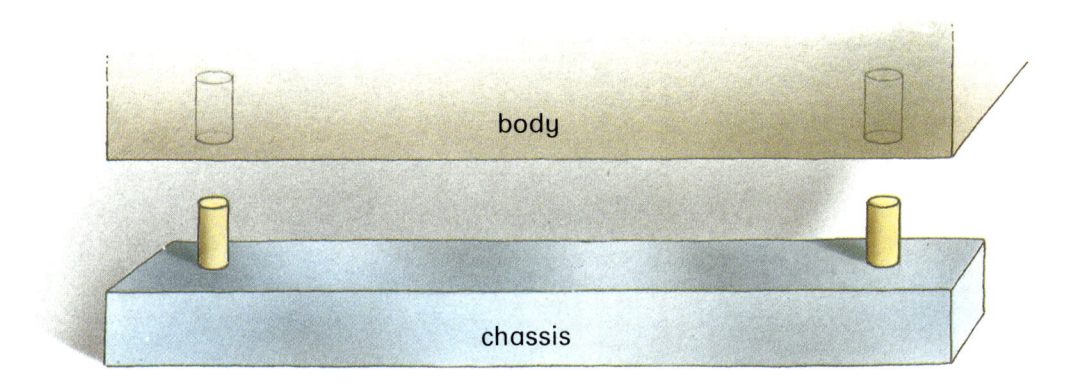

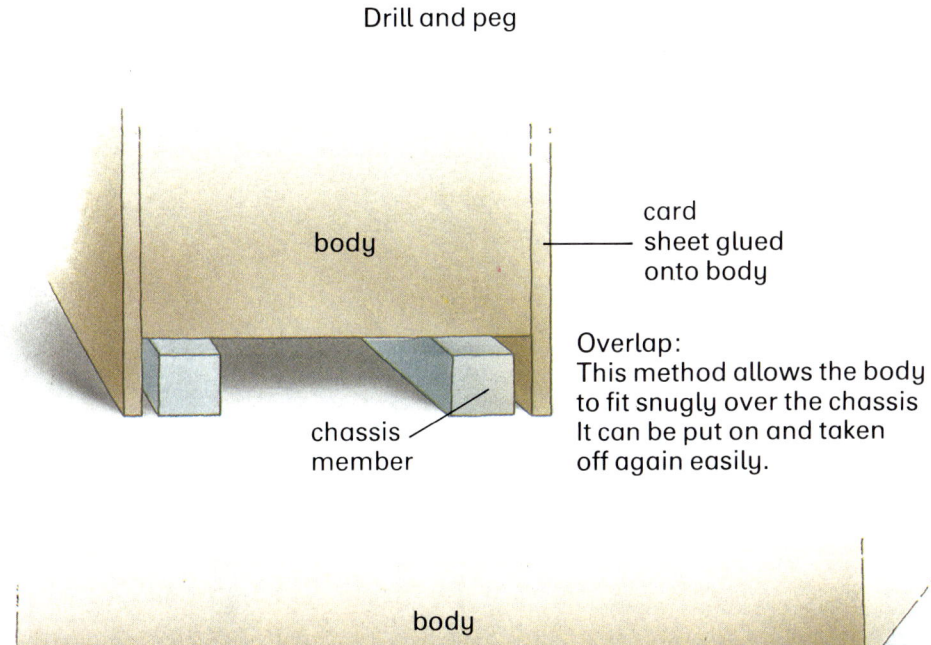

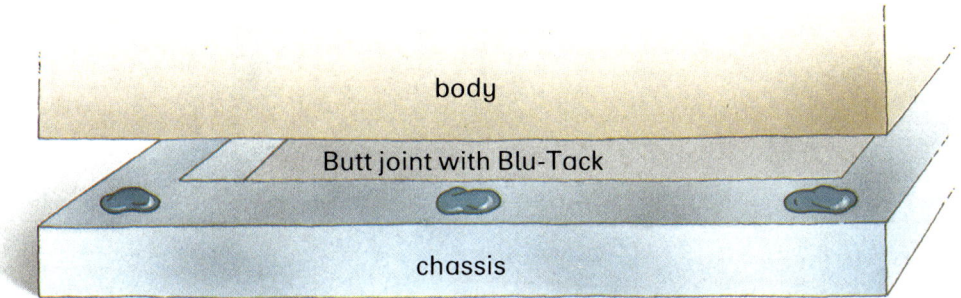

body

chassis

Drill and peg

body

card sheet glued onto body

chassis member

Overlap:
This method allows the body to fit snugly over the chassis. It can be put on and taken off again easily.

body

Butt joint with Blu-Tack

chassis

Finishes
Try different finishes.

· DATA FILE ·
Finishes

Costs

Cost your work.

Cost sheet for production line

For 10 vehicles:

	£
40 wheels at 5p	2.00
2m dowel at 5p	0.10
2 sheets card at 10p	0.20
5m square section at 5p	0.25
Blu-Tack, glue, etc	0.40
Paint transfers etc	1.00
Labour 20 hours at 20p	4.00
	£7.95

• DATA FILE •
Costing

Other ideas

Think of a name for your vehicle company and design a company logo.

How can the vehicles be packaged attractively for sale?

Show what the inside of your model vehicles would look like if they were real.

Develop an advertising campaign to sell your new vehicle.